GREAT MOMENTS IN AMERICAN HISTORY

America's Gold Rush

John Sutter and the Discovery of Gold in California

Joanne Mattern

ROSEN CENTRAL
PRIMARY SOURCE™

THE ROSEN PUBLISHING GROUP, INC., NEW YORK

Published in 2004 by The Rosen Publishing Group, Inc.
29 East 21st Street, New York, NY 10010

Editor: Geeta Sobha
Book Design: Christopher Logan
Photo researcher: Rebecca Anguin-Cohen
Series photo researcher: Jeff Wendt

Photo Credits: Cover (left), title page, p. 18 © Hulton/Archive/Getty Images; cover (right) illustration
© Debra Wainwright/The Rosen Publishing Group; p. 6 California Historical Society, FN-30892;
p. 10 California Department of Parks and Recreation; pp. 14, 29, 31, 32 © California State Library;
p. 22 © Mystic Seaport, Mystic, CT; p. 30 Courtesy of the Rare Books and Manuscripts Collection,
The New York Public Library Astor, Lenox, and Tilden Foundations

First Edition

Library of Congress Cataloging-in-Publication Data

Mattern, Joanne, 1963-
   America's gold rush : John Sutter and the discovery of gold in California /
   Joanne Mattern.— 1st ed.
   p. cm.—(Great moments in American history)
   Summary: When word leaks out that gold has been found on property owned
   by John Sutter in 1847, it changes his life and the course of American
   history forever.
   ISBN 0-8239-4365-8 (lib. bdg.)
   1. Sutter, John Augustus, 1803-1880—Juvenile literature. 2.
   Pioneers—California—Biography—Juvenile literature. 3.
   California—Gold discoveries—Juvenile literature. 4.
   California—History—1846-1850—Juvenile literature. 5. Sutter's Fort
   (Sacramento, Calif.)—Juvenile literature. [1. Sutter, John Augustus,
   1803-1880. 2. Pioneers. 3. California—Gold discoveries. 4.
   California—History—1846-1850. 5. Sutter's Fort (Sacramento, Calif.)]
   I. Title. II. Series.

   F865.S93M38 2004
   979.4'04—dc21
                                                        2003008487

Manufactured in the United States of America

CONTENTS

John Sutter came to the United States in 1834. He owed a lot of money to people in his home country of Switzerland. He left his wife and children there. They planned to join him in the United States once he made his fortune.

First, Sutter lived in Indiana. He then moved to Missouri and New Mexico to try to make money. In 1839, Sutter moved to California. At this time, Mexico owned the land of California. Sutter asked the Mexican governor for some land. He received a piece of land near the American River. Sutter started the colony of New Helvetia there. In 1841, he built Sutter's Fort.

Sutter was very friendly and got along well with people. Some people agreed to give him thousands of cows and horses, land, and other things, with

Sutter's promise to pay them back at a later date. However, once again he found himself deep in debt. Still, many people came to work for Sutter. Many of these people were Native Americans. He gave them jobs at a time when many whites would not.

In 1846, the Mexican-American War started. The United States took control of California. Sutter did not know if the Americans would let him keep the land the Mexicans gave to him. Sutter still had big plans for New Helvetia, though. He added a tannery, where leather is made, and planned to build a flour mill. He needed wood to build the flour mill. In 1847, Sutter teamed up with a carpenter named James Marshall to build a sawmill on the American River to get the wood. During the building of the sawmill, a discovery was made that changed life in the United States forever....

This 1851 photograph shows James Marshall in front of Sutter's sawmill, where Marshall found gold. Today, this area has been turned into Marshall Gold Discovery State Historic Park.

Chapter One

An Amazing Discovery

T he sun shone brightly on the afternoon of January 24, 1848. Henry Bigler took off his hat and wiped the sweat from his forehead. Though it was January, he was still very hot. Bigler and other men were building a sawmill for John Sutter near a town called Coloma on the American River. Bigler and his friend William Scott were putting the machinery in the sawmill. This was one of the last things that had to be done before the mill would work.

"Do you want something to drink?" asked Scott. He passed a canteen of water to Bigler.

"Here comes James Marshall," Scott said as he took the canteen back from Bigler. Marshall was their boss. John Sutter had hired him to be in

charge of the workers building the mill. Today, he was coming to check the tailrace. The tailrace was a 150-yard-long ditch used to carry water from the river to the sawmill's giant wheel. The power of the water moved the wheel, which moved the machinery to work the sawmill. In order for the sawmill to work properly, the water must flow freely in the tailrace.

"Hello, men!" Marshall called. "How is the work going?"

"Very well, sir," Bigler replied. "I think we're almost done."

Marshall nodded in satisfaction. "Is the water flowing well in the tailrace?" he asked.

"The water is a little deeper than it should be," Scott said. "I think some gravel is stuck in it."

Marshall walked over to the tailrace. Some shiny pebbles in the mud caught his eye. He bent down and picked them up. The tiny pebbles were yellow. Marshall's heart pounded with excitement. *Could these tiny stones be gold?* he thought.

Marshall found a heavy rock. He placed one of the yellow pebbles on the ground and hit it hard with the rock. The pebble flattened, but did not break. Marshall knew that gold was soft. Maybe he really had found gold!

"Boys, I think I have found a gold mine," Marshall whispered to Bigler and Scott. He looked at the men. "Don't tell anyone about this until I speak to John Sutter. I will leave right away," he said.

"Are you sure you want to leave right now?" asked Bigler. "Sutter's Fort is forty-five miles away and it looks like it is going to rain."

"The rain will not hurt me. I must find out if this is gold or not. There is no time to waste!" Marshall said as he wrapped the pebbles in a rag and put them in his pocket. Within minutes Marshall was on his horse and headed for Sutter's Fort. He was excited about the discovery. If the stones turned out to be gold, he could become a rich man!

When Mexico gave John Sutter land, he turned it into a settlement called New Helvetia. He wanted to make a large farming community of which he would be the leader.

Chapter Two

TESTING FOR GOLD

R ain pounded on the window of John Sutter's office. Sutter sat at his desk, writing a letter to his family. Suddenly, the door to his office flew open. In the doorway stood John Marshall, soaking wet and breathing heavily. "What is the matter, John?" Sutter asked. "You left here only two days ago. Has something happened at the mill?"

"I have some information for you that may make us both very rich," Marshall announced excitedly.

"What is it?" Sutter asked.

"Can we go to your private room? No one must hear what I have to tell you," Marshall replied.

"Okay, but the only other person in the building is a clerk. He's working in his office," Sutter said as he rose from his chair. "My room is this way. Follow me."

When they entered Sutter's private room, Sutter took a seat. "Please, sit down. Or at least tell me what it is you are so excited about," he said.

Marshall reached into his pocket and pulled out the rag in which he had placed the pebbles he found. As he was untying the small package, the door to the room opened. Sutter's clerk stood in the doorway. Marshall jammed the rag back into his pocket.

"Excuse me, sir. I'm sorry, I did not know you had a guest. I will come back later," the clerk said.

"Yes, I will come to your office once Mr. Marshall and I are finished," Sutter said.

"Do you think he saw anything?" Marshall asked when the clerk had left.

"I'm sure he didn't, James," Sutter replied. "I know *I* didn't see anything. What is it that you have there?"

Marshall walked over to the door and locked it. He pulled the rag out of his pocket again. He held out the shiny pebbles he had taken from the tailrace for Sutter to see.

"Is that gold?" Sutter asked, his eyes wide with excitement.

"I think it is," Marshall said.

Sutter took a large encyclopedia from his bookcase. "There are several tests for gold in this encyclopedia," he said. "Let's try them and see if we will soon be rich men!"

For the next several hours, Marshall and Sutter tested the gold. They pounded it with a hammer. They weighed the pebbles. They even poured acid on them to see if the pebbles would dissolve. The pebbles passed every test. Sutter smiled. "I think you have found gold!" he said.

"We should go to the sawmill right away," Marshall said.

"Let's leave in the morning. It is nearly dinnertime now. No gold will be found tonight," Sutter said.

"You can wait for tomorrow morning. I'll go ahead and make sure that all is well at the mill," Marshall said, putting on his hat.

After Marshall had left, Sutter sat back in his chair and looked at the gold. He wondered how this discovery was going to change his life.

The page shown above is from San Francisco's *Pacific News*, October 9, 1849. It is a letter written by Sutter that tells of Marshall's gold discovery.

Chapter Three

THE BIG SECRET

S utter and a Native American worker left for the sawmill at 7:00 A.M. the next morning. They traveled about 22 miles through rain. Suddenly, they saw a man crawl from beneath a bush. "Who is that?" Sutter asked his worker.

"I think it's the man who came to visit you yesterday," the worker replied.

Sutter could see now that it was Marshall. "James!" he yelled. "Why are you sleeping on the side of the road?"

"I made it to the sawmill and all was well. I turned back last night to meet you," he said.

"You should have just stayed with me last night," Sutter said. "You'll get sick staying out here in the rain."

The men rode the rest of the way to the sawmill.

The next morning, Sutter followed Marshall to the tailrace. The water had been stopped from running through the tailrace so that some gravel could be cleaned out of it. Sutter took off his shoes, rolled up his pants, and stepped into the tailrace. Immediately, he spotted something shining in the bottom. "James! I've found some gold," he said, holding up the small pebbles. "If it's this easy to find, we'll be rich in no time."

"Some workers have already started finding gold," Marshall replied. "It is everywhere."

The next day, Sutter went looking for gold with Marshall. The two men walked along the American River and found several small pieces of shiny metal. Sutter was happy about the gold, but he knew it would not be kept a secret for long.

"I would like to talk to the men before I leave. Ask them to meet me around eight o'clock tomorrow morning," Sutter told Marshall.

The next morning, Marshall and the rest of the workers gathered around Sutter. "Thank you all

for coming," he said. "As you probably know, gold has been found here. I know that everyone is eager to get some. However, I have one large favor to ask. Please keep this discovery a secret for six weeks. This will allow me to finish my flour mill. In return, you will be among the first to get a chance to look for the gold. Does this agreement work for everyone?"

The workers nodded their heads in agreement. Sutter left shortly after finishing his speech. Even though his workers agreed to keep the discovery a secret, he was worried. If the secret got out there was no telling what might happen. He hoped that the United States would let him keep all of the land that Mexico had given him, but this had not yet happened. The Mexican-American War was still not over. Any person could come to his land and take what he or she wanted—and there was nothing Sutter could do to stop it. *There is no way a secret this big can be kept for six weeks*, he thought.

Miners used sluice boxes like the one shown here. The miners filled these long boxes with dirt, then ran water through them. The water separated the gold from the dirt.

Chapter Four

THE SECRET IS OUT

T he Mexican-American War ended nine days after Marshall discovered gold in the sawmill. By late March, Sutter still had not found out whether he would be allowed to keep his land. On March 25, 1848, Marshall once again rode into Sutter's Fort.

"Hello, James. How is everything?" greeted Sutter.

"I have some bad news," Marshall said as he got off his horse. "Our secret is out. Most of the men have stopped working on the mill. They only look for gold now. Also, hundreds of people have already come from other cities to look for gold. I've already seen these people along the river."

"Yes, I know," Sutter said, shaking his head. He pulled a folded piece of newspaper from his pocket. "I read this article from the San Francisco newspaper

today," he said as he handed the paper to Marshall. "It tells of our discovery of gold. No one will ignore news of a gold mine being found. Only two weeks after I returned from the sawmill, Mr. Smith, a store owner here in the fort, received gold as payment. Mr. Smith and his partner have now rented an even larger store from me. They have bought a lot of supplies for prospectors interested in finding gold. I don't know what to do. My flour mill is not finished. I do not think anyone will work for the pay I can offer when there is gold to be found."

"Come back to Coloma with me tomorrow," Marshall said. "Maybe you can get some of the workers there to help you with the flour mill."

"I will try," Sutter replied. "I just hope that the workers there haven't gone out looking for gold, too."

Marshall and Sutter set out the next morning for Coloma. In addition to the sawmill, Sutter also owned a tannery and many acres of wheat fields there. Sutter and Marshall went to the tannery first. "Hello? Is anyone here?" Sutter called out as he entered the tannery. The place was empty. Animal skins had been

left to rot. "Look at this mess!" Sutter cried. "All of the skins are ruined. I can't sell any of these."

Sutter and Marshall left the tannery. As they rode along the river, they passed many empty tents that belonged to the people who had worked for him. They were all out looking for gold. Sutter and Marshall rode to the wheat fields. Several Native Americans were working to break up the soil in order to plant. "Hello there," Sutter called to Maiki, the Native American in charge of the workers. "Have many men left you to find gold?" Sutter asked.

"Some have gone to find gold and many more want to go. We have heard that pieces of gold the size of eggs have been found," Maiki said.

Sutter thought for a moment. "If I cannot run my mills, I might as well try to find gold myself," he said. "Maiki, tell your workers that I will get the supplies ready and we will look for gold after the wheat harvest."

If all of these people can get rich off my land, why shouldn't I? Sutter thought.

Once word of the discovery of gold at Sutter's mill got out, people began to flock to California. This photograph shows ships that were deserted in San Francisco Bay when sailors went looking for gold.

Chapter Five

THE END OF SUTTER

I n September 1848, Sutter brought his son, Johann Augustus Sutter Jr., called August, from Switzerland. He gave his son ownership of most of his land. Sutter wanted his son to manage his land while he searched for gold.

Sutter and many of his Native American workers camped in the mountains around the American River. They found some gold, but everywhere they went there were others also looking for gold. Sutter moved from place to place. He tried to find a spot that wasn't already crowded with gold prospectors. However, he did not succeed. Too many people knew about the gold. In 1849, Sutter gave up looking for gold. He sold Sutter's Fort to pay some of his growing debt. He moved with his son to his farm, Hock Farm, near the Feather River in California.

On a chilly day in February 1850, Sutter sat on the porch of the main house at Hock Farm. He was in a bad mood. His wife and other children were on their way from Switzerland to join him at Hock Farm. He had wanted them to have the finest furniture and clothes when they joined him. He thought of the wealth he had lost and the many debts he now had. He could not afford to give his family everything he wanted to. When Sutter looked up, he saw his son walking toward him. August had just arrived from doing business in Sacramento, California.

"Good morning, Father," August said as he stepped onto the porch.

"Good morning, August," Sutter replied. "How was your trip?"

August frowned and sat down next to his father. "I don't think it went well," he said. "I sold some of our land for a good price, but I have not received any money for it yet. I am beginning to think that I won't be paid for it at all."

Sutter looked out over his farmland. "I sold several plots of land around the farm to pay for some furniture

for your mother," he said. "I am afraid I may have to sell more to get out of some of my debt. If only the gold would have been found a few years later. By then I would have been making enough money at Sutter's Fort and Coloma to pay everyone back. As it was, I was too deep in debt. I could never find enough gold to get out of it."

"Don't worry, Father," August said. "We'll get out of debt someday."

"I hope you're right," Sutter replied.

In 1850, Sutter's wife, Anna, and the rest of his children arrived. They were surprised to see how Sutter was living. They had expected him to be wealthy and well respected. Instead, he was deeply in debt and angry. Sutter gave the ownership of Hock Farm to Anna so that the people he owed money to would not take it for payment.

Sutter's troubles were not over. On June 21, 1865, someone set fire to his house on Hock Farm. Sutter then moved with his family to Washington, D.C. He had given up on making his fortune in California. While in Washington, he tried to get the government

to repay him money he had lost on his land during the gold rush. Sutter was unsuccessful and soon grew tired of living in Washington. In 1871, Sutter and Anna moved to Lititz, Pennsylvania. Sutter still traveled to Washington often to try to get the government to pay him for his losses. Sutter died on June 18, 1880. He never recovered from the losses he suffered during the gold rush and was still in debt.

The gold rush changed Sutter's life and the lives of many Americans. Thousands of people from around the world moved to California in search of gold. The number of people living in San Francisco, California, grew from about eight hundred people in 1848 to more than fifty thousand people in 1849. The gold rush also helped to shape the United States's borders. In 1850, California became the thirty-first state in the United States of America. As a result, the United States of America stretched from the Atlantic Ocean to the Pacific Ocean. The discovery of gold on John Sutter's land and the gold rush that followed changed the United States forever.

GLOSSARY

debt (DET) an amount of money or something else that you owe

dissolve (di-ZOLV) to seem to disappear when mixed with liquid

encyclopedia (en-sye-kloh-PEE-dee-uh) a book or set of books with information about many different subjects, usually arranged in alphabetical order

flour mill (FLOU-ur MIL) a building in which grain is ground into flour

gravel (GRAV-uhl) small, loose stones

harvest (HAR-vist) the gathering of crops that are ripe

prospectors (PROSS-pekt-uhrz) people who look for things, especially silver or gold

sawmill (SAW-mil) a place where people use machines to saw logs into timber

tailrace (TAYL-rayss) a long ditch that brings water to the wheel of a mill

tannery (TAN-uh-ree) a place where animal skins are turned into leather

Primary Sources

O ne way to study history is to examine primary sources. Primary sources are things such as old letters, drawings, maps, diaries, and photographs. By studying sources such as these, we can learn about the people, places, and events of the past.

The drawing by John Marshall that is shown on page 32 lets us see from his point of view how he discovered gold at Sutter's sawmill. By analyzing his drawing, we may even construct a story or an explanation of what happened on that day.

The map on page 31 allows us to draw conclusions about the discovery of gold on the growth of California. So many people were coming to find gold that maps were made to help them reach California quickly and safely.

The drawing and the map help us understand the importance of Marshall's discovery. Sources such as the examples given here are very important to understanding historical events.

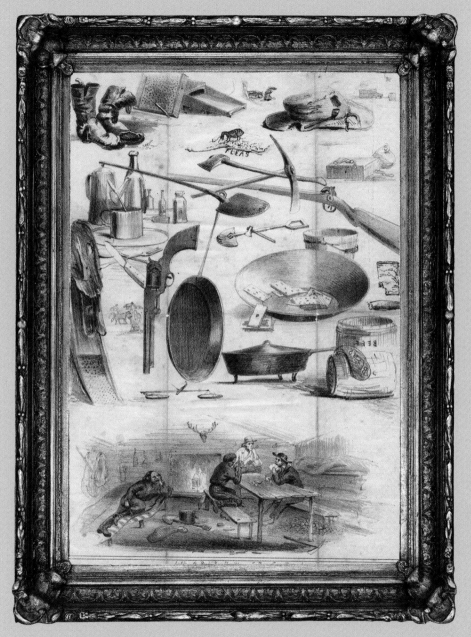

This illustration published in 1856 shows some of the items and tools miners used or carried. It also shows the inside of a typical cabin where miners lived.

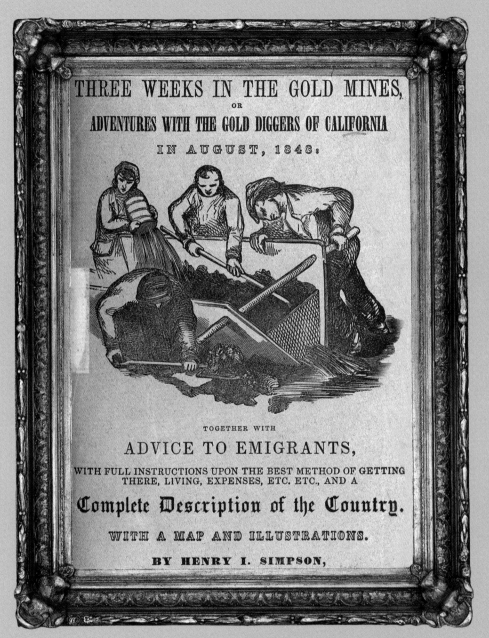

THREE WEEKS IN THE GOLD MINES,

OR

ADVENTURES WITH THE GOLD DIGGERS OF CALIFORNIA

IN AUGUST, 1848:

TOGETHER WITH

ADVICE TO EMIGRANTS,

WITH FULL INSTRUCTIONS UPON THE BEST METHOD OF GETTING
THERE, LIVING, EXPENSES, ETC. ETC., AND A

Complete Description of the Country.

WITH A MAP AND ILLUSTRATIONS.

BY HENRY I. SIMPSON,

Guidebooks like the one shown here gave prospectors useful information about finding gold in California. This book published in New York offers "full instructions upon the best methods of getting there, living, etc. etc...."

This 1849 map shows routes used by boats carrying mail. The map also shows areas where gold had been found. These areas are in yellow. Different paths to California are also shown.

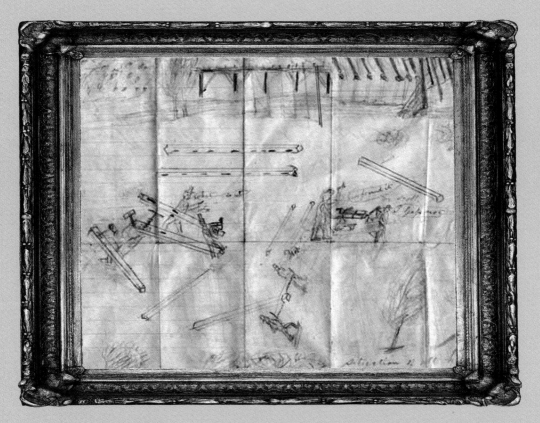

This drawing, done by James Marshall, tells of how he discovered gold at Sutter's sawmill. The figure with the raised arm on the right is Marshall. He's saying, "I have found it."